Midnight Adventure

The strange noise grew louder and louder.

'I don't like it,' whispered Tim, crouching lower into the grass. Gerry lay flat, his fish forgotten.

Suddenly a huge black shape appeared through the trees, coming straight towards them. Tim curled up into a ball, his eyes wide and staring. Gerry lay flat, clutching the grass. They were both too frightened to move.

Midnight Adventure

Written and illustrated by

Raymond Briggs

Beaver Books

A Beaver Book
Published by Arrow Books Limited
17–21 Conway Street, London W1P 6JD

An imprint of the Hutchinson Publishing Group

London · Melbourne · Sydney · Auckland
Johannesburg and agencies throughout the world

First published by Hamish Hamilton 1961
Beaver edition 1976
Reprinted 1985

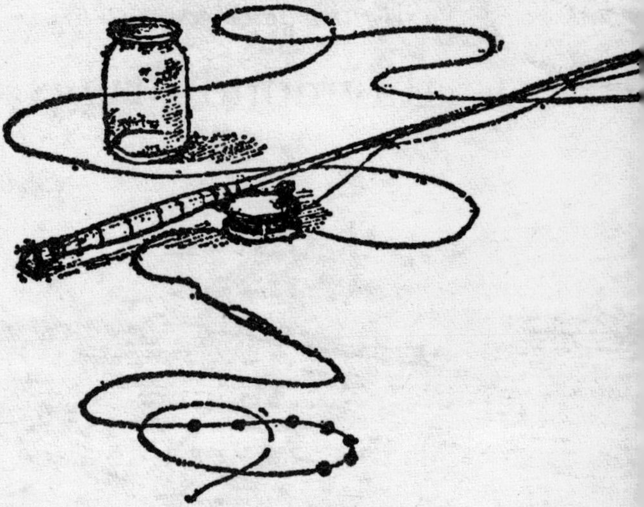

Set in Baskerville by Rowland Phototypesetting Limited
Bury St Edmunds, Suffolk
Made and printed in Great Britain by
Cox & Wyman Limited, Reading

ISBN 0 09 941870 3

Contents

Chapter One

Plans for Midnight

Gerry Martin and his friend Tim Rogers had planned to go out fishing at night, so they were now digging for worms in Tim's garden.

'My it's hot!' puffed Tim, raising his fork in one hand and driving it into the ground like a spear. He lay down in the grass and looked up through the leaves of the apple tree.

'Come on,' said Gerry, still digging vigorously. 'We haven't got half enough yet.'

'Yes, we have,' replied Tim as he rolled over to watch the wriggling tangle in the jam jar. 'Because I've decided to use bread crust instead. Float it out on the surface with a size sixteen hook. That's what my Uncle Bob does and he is a real carp expert.'

'Well, I'm sticking to worms,' said Gerry, 'and I bet I catch more carps than you do.'

'I bet you don't, and besides there's no "s" on carp either. You'll be talking about sheeps next.'

'Here, Mr Knowall. Have a worm,' said Gerry as he lightly tossed one over at Tim's face.

Tim ducked and rolled away, then jumped up and threw himself on to Gerry's back.

They fell to the ground, with Tim on top tearing up handfuls of grass and stuffing them down Gerry's neck.

'Stop it!' cried Gerry. 'The grass is full of insects. I'll be bitten to death.'

'They'll only join up with those you've already got,' replied Tim, pushing his knee under Gerry's

chin and tickling his nose with a bunch of grass.

Gerry flung his head to one side, 'Look out! You've knocked the worms over. They're all getting away.'

In a moment both boys were on their feet and hurriedly gathering up the escaping worms.

'There'll be enough,' said Tim, when the worms were safely in the jar again. 'You can have them all as I'm using bread.'

'All right, thanks, Tim,' said Gerry, as he pulled himself up into the apple tree. 'Let's work out what we're going to do tonight.'

Tim joined him in the tree, and they settled into their favourite places.

'How are you going to get in and out if you can't borrow a door key?' asked Tim.

'Oh, it's easy. I just get out of my window, then along the kitchen roof and down the pipe. I've done it hundreds of times. Is your sister still going to lend you her key?'

'Yes,' replied Tim, 'Pat's pretty good considering she's only a girl.'

'I know,' said Gerry, 'I wish I had a sister like

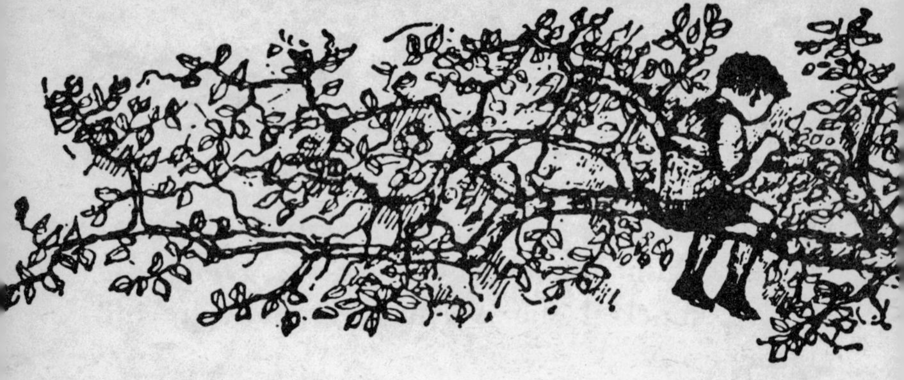

that. My brother is useless. It's just like having three parents.'

'What time shall we meet?' asked Tim.

'Midnight,' said Gerry, 'in the alley by the tunnel.'

'I wish there was some other way into the park,' said Tim. 'I don't fancy that tunnel at night. I've a good mind to cross the railway line instead.'

'No, that's much too dangerous,' replied Gerry. 'You know the park railings are too high to climb, so the tunnel where the stream goes under the railway embankment is the only way. I know! Let's make a plan. Could you ask your mother for some paper, Tim?'

'I suppose so,' said Tim, 'if you must always work everything out to the last detail.'

He ran indoors, and a few moments later came back with pencils and paper and a book to rest the paper on.

Gerry at once took charge of everything.

'Now the Plan,' he said importantly.

'The great General Martin on the battlefield!' announced Tim, jumping to attention and doing an exaggerated salute.

'Quiet,' said Gerry sternly as he frowned at the paper. 'What shall we call it?'

'Uncle Timmy and Auntie Gerry go fishing,' suggested Tim, as he swung on a branch.

'Oh, shut up, Tim. This is an important plan, not a book for tiny tots like you.'

Gerry crouched down over the paper, muttering the words to himself as he wrote, 'MIDNIGHT FISHING EXPEDITION – NUMBER ONE.'

Tim was now sitting in the tree again, gazing

up at the sky and humming to himself as he swung his feet to and fro.

Gerry hunched over the paper, filling it from edge to edge with dense lines of writing.

'We're only going fishing, you know,' said Tim. 'We're not going to climb Mount Everest or something.'

Gerry was so deep in his plans he did not even hear. Muttering and grunting to himself, he wrote on and on. There were long lists of things to bring, and a detailed plan of the action. Finally the back of the paper was covered with a map of the whole district.

'There, that's it,' he said at last, as he handed the paper up to Tim.

Tim brought his gaze down from the sky, and tried to fix it on the closely packed scribble.

'Mmm, clear as mud. Yes, and what is this about mud here?'

'There's mud in the tunnel,' said Gerry. 'Ronny Davis and I were going to build stepping stones all through once, but we never finished it. The point is that we can use it to darken our faces, so that we won't be seen if there are any keepers about in the park.'

'Oh, I see now,' said Tim. 'Terrible writing. Childish, that's what it is, childish. You know, if we're caught near the tea pavilion at that time of night, with mud on our faces and torches, they'll think we're those burglars everyone's been talking about.'

'Oh, don't be silly,' said Gerry. 'They've been emptying whole houses, furniture, carpets and everything, with a great lorry. You forget you're just a tiny little boy, Master Timothy Rogers.'

'I'm a good inch taller than you, you little shrimp,' said Tim, jumping out of the tree.

'You are *not*!' cried Gerry, raising himself to his full height.

'I AM!' shouted Tim, straining up on tip-toe.

'NOT!' shouted Gerry, and flung himself on to Tim. They fought furiously in the sun for a few

minutes, a writhing bundle of punching fists and poking elbows.

'Oh, it's too hot,' gasped Tim. 'I give up.'

'So do I,' said Gerry, rolling away. 'You're not worth bashing, you're too easy.'

'It's only because I don't try,' puffed Tim. 'I'm frightened of hurting you, you little weed.'

They lay on their backs in the sun, panting for breath.

'Look,' said Gerry, 'we'd better put a pillow in our beds to look as if we're still in them, just in case anyone looks in.'

'Yes,' replied Tim, 'and I was going to say we ought to leave a note, too, in case they find out we're not there. Pat's going to be away, and my mother would start telephoning the police straight away if I was missing.'

'Yes, good idea,' said Gerry. 'We could leave it with the pillow. Shall I write yours for you, or do you think you can manage?'

'I came first in English last term,' said Tim. 'Where were you? Nineteenth, wasn't it?'

A voice called from the house. 'Tim! Dinner's ready.' It was his mother.

'Coming,' Tim answered.

'Yes, I've got to go, too,' said Gerry, jumping up. 'Look, we're going out all the afternoon and evening, so I shan't see you till tonight. You keep the plan, because I can remember it. You'd better bring the worms, too, as they're here.'

'All right,' said Tim, as he looked at the plan again. 'Well, I never! The great General Martin has left something off the list.'

'Oh? What?' asked Gerry huffily.

'The fishing tackle,' laughed Tim.

'Oh, well, even a nitwit like you shouldn't need reminding of that.'

'See you at midnight, then,' said Tim, walking away.

Gerry jumped up on to the fence. 'Yes. Cheerio,

and don't be late,' he called as he dropped down out of sight.

'Cheerio,' said Tim, and ran into dinner.

Chapter Two

Midnight Expedition

That night Tim lay awake excitedly waiting for midnight. He had laid out under the bed all the things he needed to take. His rod, reel, landing-net, keep-net, tackle bag of weights, casts and hooks, and the worms. He had sorted out all his darkest clothes, and had tested the stairs to see which ones creaked.

He lay in bed playing with a huge silver torch he had been given for his birthday. It held three big batteries and had a press-button switch for morse signalling. When the end was twisted, it made either a wide beam which lit up the whole room, or a long, narrow beam which spotlighted things three hundred feet away.

The moment he heard his parents coming up the stairs, he switched off the torch and ducked under the bedclothes in case his mother looked in.

After they had gone safely to bed, Tim could wait no longer. He jumped out of bed and began pulling on his clothes. In a few seconds he was dressed and ready to go.

He sat on a chair by the window and looked out. Then he got up and walked to the door. He put his hand on the knob, then went back and sat on the bed, his hands gripping his knees and his feet tapping up and down with impatience.

The church clock at the end of the street struck eleven. 'Oh, it can't be,' groaned Tim. 'Another hour! I'll have to get back into bed in case anyone comes in.'

He undressed, put his pyjamas on again, then climbed back into bed and lay there staring at the ceiling.

After a while he picked up the torch again and began spotlighting things round the room. Then he shone it on his feet under the bedclothes. This

made him feel he was in a tent or cave, so he took an old walking stick from under the bed and wedged it under the bedclothes as a tent pole. He then sat in his tent trying to read, but was far too excited.

Finally Tim curled round the tent pole, singing and whistling to himself to pass the time, and switching his torch off and on in time to the music.

After what seemed hours, the clock struck twelve. Tim leaped out of bed, and hurriedly dressed again. He put a pillow, together with the note for his mother, just inside the covers; then gathered up his things and tip-toed to the door.

Gripping the handle firmly, he twisted it slowly to the left, praying for it not to click.

The door opened quietly, and Tim closed it carefully behind him. He crept down the stairs, taking care to tread only on the sides and not in the middle, to prevent them from creaking. He tip-toed up the hall to the front door, opened it gently and closed it slowly and carefully behind him.

There was a loud click as it shut, then Tim ran across the garden, swung round the gate-post, and out into the deserted street.

His footsteps sounded loud in the silence, and the rustle of the trees, almost unnoticed in the day time, made it seem as if the sea was just behind the houses. The leaves cast moving shadows on the pavement.

Meanwhile Gerry, who had waited just as impatiently as Tim, climbed down from his window and set off as fast as he could for the alleyway.

The two boys arrived almost at the same time and went into the darkness of the alleyway together. 'Got the bait and everything?' asked Gerry.

'Yes, I checked it all off on the list,' said Tim. 'Let's push the rods through the fence before we get over.' They hung their bags on the fence, pushed their rods through, and climbed over.

Gerry reached down into the stream and lifted out a handful of mud. He squeezed it almost dry and began smearing it on his face. 'Here, Tim, have some.'

Tim put down the bags and dipped his fingers in the mud. 'You don't need much,' said Gerry as Tim began plastering it on. 'Just one or two smears to break up the shape of your face.'

'Look out!' cried Tim suddenly. He pushed Gerry backwards into the grass as a train rattled along the top of the embankment. Its windows shone patches of light down the slope, and Tim and Gerry lay still as the light flashed over them.

'We're in full view of those houses,' whispered Tim.

'Oh, they'll all be asleep by now,' replied Gerry, as the train faded into the distance. 'Let's get into the stream.'

They picked up their rods and stepped into the

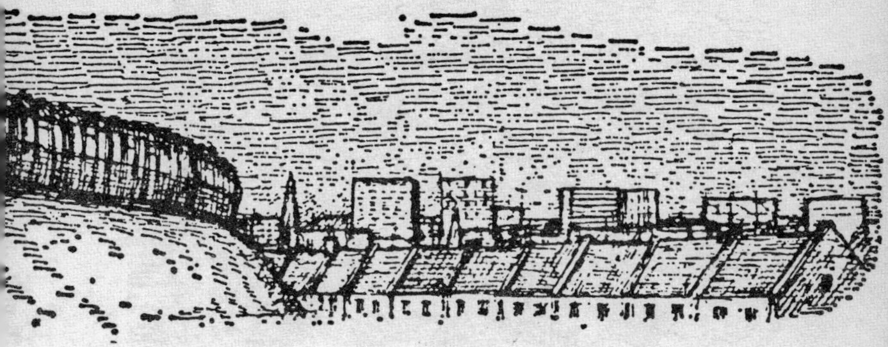

water. 'My, it's oozy,' said Tim. 'It's like walking in treacle.'

'I know,' agreed Gerry. 'There's only four or five inches of water, the rest is all mud.' They paddled into the tunnel mouth and switched on their torches. Tim's powerful beam lit up the whole tunnel and made the ripples at the far end glitter.

Their wellingtons made loud sucking noises as they pulled them up out of the mud and moved deeper into the tunnel. 'It's hard work,' said Tim. 'I'm hot already.'

'We're about half way now,' said Gerry. 'It's not much further.'

Suddenly there was a loud roar and the whole tunnel shook.

'It's collapsing!' cried Tim.

They clung desperately to one another as the roaring and shaking grew louder and louder.

Then, as it gradually died away, Gerry sighed with relief. 'Oh, of course, it's only a train.'

Tim's throat felt so tight he could hardly speak. 'Let's go on then,' he whispered.

The water lapped loudly and eerily about them as they paddled on, steadying themselves with shaking arms against the slippery walls of the tunnel. Gradually the dim glow of moonlight at the far end drew nearer. The ripples from their wellingtons travelled ahead of them, out of the tunnel mouth and into the moonlight. Then a moment later, they were through.

A cool breeze blew on their faces, and the

slapping echo of the water softened into the rustling of leaves.

'Oh, thank goodness for that,' said Tim, sitting down on the bank as his knees almost gave way with relief.

'Come on, we can't sit about,' said Gerry. He crouched under the bushes and waded on up the stream.

Tim slowly stood up and followed him.

'Here's a bridge,' said Gerry. 'Duck under.'

They crawled under the bridge and went on through the bushes again.

'This is where we get out,' said Gerry, as they came to the tea pavilion. They lay on the bank, well hidden in the bushes, listening intently.

'Can't hear anything,' whispered Tim.

'No, I think it's all right.' Gerry ran on tip-toe across the path and vanished into the shadow of the hedge. Tim followed silently, and together they crept past the tea pavilion, jumped the low, wooden fence, and ran up the slope to the lake.

'What about going just the other side of those railings?' said Gerry, as they saw them through the trees.

'That's the golf course woods,' Tim replied.

'Yes, but it's where they all fish,' said Gerry. 'It's deeper there.'

'All right,' said Tim. 'Give me your rod, I'll put them through.'

'There are horrible great spikes on the end,' Gerry whispered. 'Mind your wellingtons.'

Tim followed Gerry out over the lake, holding on to the curving spikes and standing on the very edge of the rail with just the tips of his toes. The row of iron spikes was only an inch or two from his face as he swung round the end. Gerry handed Tim his rod as he landed, and they crept quietly on through the bushes.

'Here we are,' whispered Gerry, as he came to the edge of the lake again.

The bank curved gently round in a wide bay, and the moon shone on the deep, quiet water. A faint breeze made the trees rustle, and suddenly the moon's reflection was broken, making it dance on the tiny ripples. All at once, Tim wished he was safely home in bed. Gerry was silent, too, as they watched the moon in the water slowly fitting itself together again.

'Come on,' said Gerry briskly, 'let's get the rods ready.'

A few moments later, Gerry put a worm on his hook and cast quietly out into the lake. He propped the rod on its rests, pulled down the line between two rings, and squeezed a lump of bread paste on to it. Then he lay down, with his head in his hands, and stared at the hanging white blob.

Tim flicked his bread out on to the surface and sat watching the little white dot as the dark rings of the ripples spread wider and wider from it, making the moon wobble and break again.

Chapter Three

The Black Shape

Tim and Gerry lay still, silently watching their lines in the moonlight. There was no sound but the faint rustle of the trees, and the occasional plop of a fish coming to the surface.

Tim looked at the moonlight shining on the bright beads of dew in the long grass, and at the black reflections of trees in the water. The cold moonlight and the hard glitter in the darkness made him feel small and lonely. Again he wished he was at home in bed, in the warm ordinariness of his own room.

After half an hour Gerry suddenly whispered, 'I think there's something on, look!' Tim turned round and watched the dangling lump of paste on Gerry's line as it rose slightly, then fell gently back again.

'He's sniffing round it,' said Gerry in an excited whisper.

'My uncle says they sometimes do that for ages before they take it,' said Tim, glancing back at his own bait.

'I know, you can't strike until they run.'

'Listen! What's that noise?' whispered Tim. 'That funny crackling sound. Hear it?' Gerry raised his head to listen, with his eyes still on the lump of paste. 'Yes, it's coming nearer.'

The strange noise grew louder and louder.

'I don't like it,' whispered Tim, crouching lower into the grass. Gerry lay flat, his fish forgotten.

Suddenly a huge black shape appeared through the trees, coming straight towards them. Tim curled up into a ball, his eyes wide and staring. Gerry lay flat, clutching the grass. They were both too frightened to move.

The crackling shape came rushing nearer and nearer, then swerved and swept past them, brushing back the leaves and branches.

'Oh!' cried Tim. 'Whatever is it?'

Gerry jumped up and stared after the vanishing shape. 'It's a lorry,' he said. 'It's going downhill with its lights and engine off. That crackling was its tyres on the gravel.'

'I didn't know we were so near the drive,' said Tim.

'Nor did I, but what's it doing here at this time of night? It's past one o'clock.'

'Oh, never mind, I expect it's the golf club people doing something. Why worry? They couldn't have seen us.' Tim turned back to watch his bread crust.

'They must be up to something with their lights and engine switched off,' said Gerry.

'Well, let's creep along and see what's happening.'

'I'll have to leave my fish, then,' said Gerry, kneeling down to look at the paste on his line. 'You go.'

'No fear,' cried Tim, 'not on my own.'

'I think he's gone anyway,' said Gerry, looking at the motionless line. 'The lorry frightened him off, I expect, so I'll come with you as you're scared.'

They wound in their lines and stood their rods against a tree, then crept quietly through the woods towards the golf club.

'I can see it now,' whispered Gerry as he peered through the leaves. 'The lorry is outside the main door, look.' Tim came up close to Gerry and they both looked out at the strangely quiet scene.

Dark and silent figures moved like shadows in and out of the club house, carrying things up a ramp into the lorry and stowing them away soundlessly.

A television set was carried out and the moonlight shone briefly on its blank, staring eye, making it blink at them. Then the four men went in together and came out carrying a gleaming refrigerator, looking like an immense block of ice in the moonlight.

'You know who they are, don't you?' asked Gerry.

'Yes, they're the burglars all right. And we've caught them red-handed. There'll be nothing left in a minute,' said Tim.

A moment later a man came out with his arms full of silver cups.

'Look, treasure!' cried Tim.

'Ssh,' hissed Gerry, 'don't be silly. It's only golf trophies.'

'We'd better do something,' Tim went on. 'They'll be taking up the floor boards next, and the glass out of the windows.'

'Yes, but if we go back through the tunnel they'll be gone before we can get the police.'

'The lorry must be almost full already,' said Tim. 'There's a man bringing out a roll of carpet.'

'We'd better creep nearer and try and get the number,' said Gerry.

They dropped flat and wriggled out from the cover of the wood. 'The grass is soaking,' whispered Tim.

'Ssh,' said Gerry.

They crept through the grass, keeping close to the bank beside the road. Gerry finally crawled up

the bank behind a bush, and rolled into a ditch only a few yards from the lorry. Tim followed and lowered himself into the ditch just behind Gerry.

Their clothes were soaked through at the knees and elbows, and they shivered as they watched more and more things being piled into the lorry.

'Gerry,' whispered Tim, crawling nearer and lying on top of him to whisper in his ear. 'We could use the club telephone if they leave the door open.'

'Yes, good idea,' grunted Gerry. 'Get off me, for goodness' sake.'

'That's about it,' said one of the men, coming out with his arms full of bottles. 'Here we are, mates, a little light refreshment after a hard night's work.' The other men laughed, one shut the door of the club house while the others silently raised

the tailboard of the lorry, then all four climbed into the cab and quietly closed the doors.

'Blow it,' said Gerry. 'They've shut the door and I still can't see the number.'

The engine started and the lorry rolled forward.

'I *must* see the number,' said Gerry, jumping to his feet and running after the lorry.

He came up quite close to it, but still could not make out the figures on the mud-covered number plate. Almost before he knew what he was doing, he had caught hold of the back and hauled himself up.

Tim watched for a second, then raced after the lorry, keeping to the left of it to avoid being seen in the driver's mirror. He soon caught it up, as it was still moving slowly, and Gerry helped him up into the back.

'Did they see you?'

'No, they'd have stopped by now if they had,' panted Tim. 'Whatever did you go and get on for?'

'I don't know. I couldn't see the number – so I just got on.'

'Oh, you are an idiot,' said Tim.

'Well, you got on, too.'

'Yes, but only to stay with you.'

They sat down in the tiny, cramped space by the tailboard as the lorry crawled on up the drive. 'We'd better watch out for a policeman, and call out if we see one,' said Tim.

'Yes,' replied Gerry, 'or jump off just before we arrive where we're going.'

Soon the lorry stopped and someone got down to unlock the gates. The boys ducked low as the lorry drove past him. Then the gates were locked again. The driver switched on the lights and the lorry roared away into the darkness, with Tim and Gerry still aboard.

'Well, that's the end of our fishing anyway,' Tim said. 'I wonder what's going to happen to us now.'

Chapter Four

In the Cabinet

Tim and Gerry crouched down in the back of the speeding lorry, clinging on tightly as it swayed from side to side. Street lamps flashed past overhead, and the road seemed to rush out from beneath them. The noise of the engine was loud in

the empty streets.

Mile after mile they drove on, and the boys felt that home was slipping further and further away. They had left the streets they knew far behind, and were now in a part of London they had never seen before.

After almost an hour, Tim whispered, 'I'm lost. Where are we now?'

'I don't know,' said Gerry, 'but we must be in the docks somewhere. You can see the cranes above the houses.'

They drove down a long, narrow street of high buildings, then suddenly turned off into a still narrower side street.

'We're slowing down,' said Gerry. 'Get ready to jump.'

They rose shakily to their feet, and steadied themselves by holding on to one another.

'I've got pins and needles,' whispered Tim.

'So have I,' replied Gerry. 'I can hardly stand.'

Suddenly the lorry swerved to the right, throwing the boys on to the floor. It swept under a low arch and on between wooden doors, then skidded to a stop inside a warehouse.

'We can't get out now,' Gerry whispered. 'They'll see us with these lights on.'

'We must hide,' said Tim, looking desperately about him.

'Look! In here,' said Gerry, opening the door of a cabinet.

Tim quickly opened the other door, and they both wriggled inside and closed the doors after them.

Still no one got out of the cab, although the engine had stopped.

Then Tim and Gerry heard voices.

'Come on, get out!' said one voice from the cab.

'We can't, Jim,' came a reply. 'Taff's asleep.'

'Oh, trust him. Taff! Wake up, you lazy lump. We're all just as tired as you are.'

'All right, all right,' mumbled Taff sleepily, as he opened the door on his side.

Tim and Gerry heard the burglars climb down and slowly make their way to the back of the lorry.

They heard a loud yawn just outside the cabinet. Then, with a rattle of chains, the tailboard dropped down.

'The cabinet first,' ordered Jim.

They felt the cabinet being dragged forward, rise in the air, and then come heavily down on to the ground.

'What a weight!' said one of the men.

'Feels twice as heavy as when we put it on,' grumbled another.

'Just shows we're all worn out,' said Taff. 'Can't we leave this till morning, Jim?'

'Taff, you're just about the most idle burglar I've ever had the rotten luck to work with.'

'I can't help feeling tired, can I?' whined Taff.

'Tired? Mate, you were born tired. It's only the thought of the next lot of food that keeps you awake. All right. Leave it,' Jim ended in a disgusted voice. 'Up to beddy-byes, you little babies. Uncle Jim will be up in a minute to tuck you all in.'

Tim and Gerry heard the lorry's doors being banged shut. The sound of footsteps grew fainter.

Then there was silence. They were alone, locked in a strange warehouse with a lot of stolen goods, miles from home.

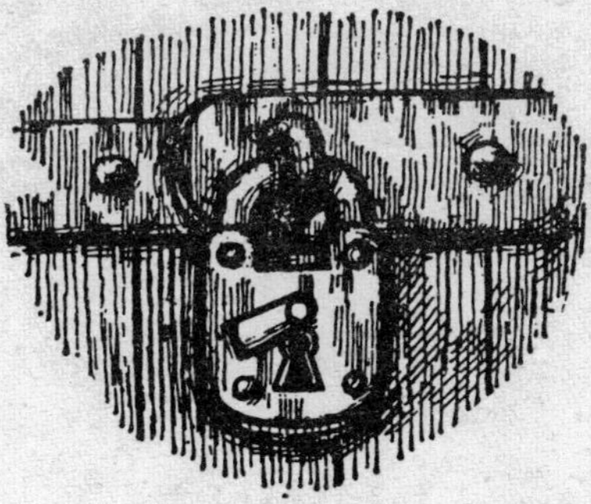

Chapter Five

Trapped

Tim tried to speak, but his mouth was dry and his throat so stiff, he produced only a frog-like croak. At last he managed to whisper, 'What are we going to do now?'

'Wait for them to fall asleep,' replied Gerry hoarsely. 'Then see about escaping.'

They sat back in silence, their feet touching, unable to see anything in the darkness.

'We'd better open the doors,' said Gerry, 'or we'll suffocate.'

When this was done they lay back again, with Gerry counting the minutes on his luminous watch.

After what seemed about an hour, Tim whispered, 'How long have we been now?'

'About twenty minutes.'

'Is that all? Oh, let's get out. They must be asleep by now.'

'All right,' agreed Gerry. 'They were all tired out, so they should be.'

They pushed the doors open wide and silently stood up. It was still very dark, but some light came in through a window high up in the roof.

'There's no way of getting out,' whispered Tim as they looked round the long, empty room. 'That sky-light is too high up to get out by.'

They tip-toed over to the door. 'No key,' said Gerry. 'They must have taken it up with them.'

'Well, there's nothing left then,' said Tim hopelessly. 'We'll just have to sit here and wait till they come down and murder us in the morning.'

'There's one thing we could do,' said Gerry, looking very serious and staring into space.

'Well, go on,' said Tim. 'What is it?'

'Start the lorry and bash the doors down with it.'

Tim looked at him incredulously. 'Have you gone potty?'

'No,' said Gerry, still very serious and thoughtful.

'But *we* can't drive a lorry, you lunatic,' cried Tim.

'Ssh! *I* can,' said Gerry, 'or at least I know how

to.' Tim stared at him again, but was too surprised and puzzled to say anything more.

'Let's get in the cab,' said Gerry, standing up. He climbed up on to the step, quietly opened the door, and disappeared inside. Tim followed silently, still wondering if Gerry had gone mad.

The air in the stuffy cab was heavy with the smells of seat leather, cigarette smoke and petrol. The battered metal floor was still hot from the engine.

'Close the door quietly,' said Gerry, looking very small beside the big steering wheel.

Tim closed the door and sat gazing at Gerry as

he stretched his legs out for the pedals. 'Thought so,' Gerry muttered, 'too far away. I hope there's a seat adjuster.' He got up from the seat and looked down beside it. 'Yes, there is. Good.'

He raised the lever and pushed the seat forward as far as it would go. 'That's better,' he said, as he lowered the lever again.

Tim just sat watching, too amazed to say anything.

'Lucky he left the ignition key,' said Gerry. 'No need for the choke, as it's still warm. Now, I'd better make sure I know what to do. It's got to work first time or they'll be down here before we're out. I mustn't stall it.'

Gerry began rehearsing the motions.

'Turn ignition key. Engine starts. Clutch down, that's the left pedal. Put in first gear. Accelerator down as I let clutch up, release hand-brake–and we're off.'

'Nothing to it,' said Tim, more bewildered than ever.

'It's quite a few yards to the doors,' said Gerry, 'so we should be going fast enough to give them a good bash by the time we get there.'

Tim nodded silently.

'Now,' Gerry went on, 'I can't drive well enough to go on when we're out in the road, and anyway, by then the crooks will be awake and down the stairs. So as soon as we're through, jump and run for it. We'd better split up in case they chase us.'

'We'll run for a phone box, shall we?' asked Tim.

'That's it,' said Gerry. 'Dial nine-nine-nine. And keep a lookout for street names as you're running, so you can tell the police where you are. Now is that everything?'

'I hope so,' said Tim crossing his fingers.

'Right then,' said Gerry, 'here goes.'

Chapter Six

The Good Bash

Tim gripped the edge of the seat and bit his lip as Gerry, his face pale and tense, took hold of the ignition key.

Then suddenly his confidence vanished. His arm felt weak and shaky and his fingers were slippery with perspiration. He let go of the key and curled up on the seat sobbing, 'I can't do it, I'm too scared.'

'Come on,' said Tim, feeling more confident

now that Gerry was nervous. 'You've just done the rehearsal. You'll be all right.'

After a few moments Gerry looked up again. 'I know. I'm all right now. Here goes!'

He reached for the key and turned it. The engine roared deafeningly, and Gerry switched on the powerful headlamps as the whole cab shook with vibration.

In some way the noise drove away their fear. 'Here we go!' yelled Gerry as he pushed the gear lever forward. He pressed the accelerator down, the engine roared louder still and blue smoke

poured out behind. Gerry let in the clutch, eased off the hand-brake and they moved forward. 'Hooray!' yelled Tim, stamping his feet with excitement. 'Faster! Faster!'

Gerry bent over the great steering wheel, gripping it with all his might. He pressed harder still on the accelerator and they charged forward. The doors came rushing closer, the headlamps reflecting dazzlingly in the shiny paintwork.

'Look out!' shouted Gerry, ducking behind the wheel.

CRASH!

The doors burst open and pieces of wood flew into the air. The padlock hit the windscreen and made a splintering star.

'How do you stop?' screamed Gerry in a panic, as they roared across the pavement and into the road.

The opposite wall seemed to rush towards them.

Suddenly Gerry remembered, took his foot off the accelerator and stamped on the brake and clutch. Tim seized the hand-brake.

As Gerry wrenched the wheel round they bumped up the kerb and skidded across the pavement, hitting a street lamp. A corner of the bumper crumpled against the wall, a headlamp shattered and there was a screech of metal as the mudguard tore against the bricks. The windscreen crackled into a pattern of frosty stars.

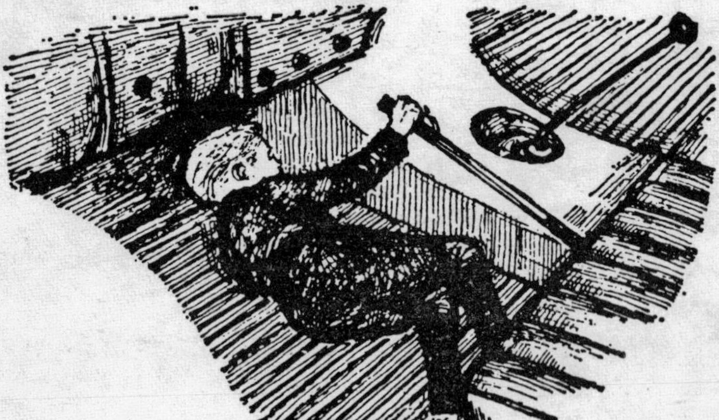

Gerry gave a gasp of pain as he was flung forward on to the steering wheel. Tim was thrown on to the floor, still clinging to the hand-brake.

The roar of the engine died away and suddenly everything was quiet. There was only the sound of petrol pouring out on to the pavement.

Tim groaned as he lay huddled on the floor. Then slowly raising himself up, he looked over at Gerry who was lying across the wheel with tears streaming down his face.

'Are you all right?' Tim whispered, as he held his own throbbing head in his hands.

'Yes, yes – I'm only winded,' gasped Gerry. 'Run for the police, I'll follow you –'

Tim looked anxiously at Gerry for a moment, then opened the door and jumped down from the cab. He landed in the puddle of petrol and glanced round behind him.

The smashed doors of the warehouse were gaping open. A trail of furniture and carpets had fallen out from the back of the lorry and stretched across the road to the wrecked vehicle. The refrigerator lay in the midst of it all, its door hanging open and its ice cubes scattered over the road.

Two large salmon had rolled out of it and lay glistening and silvery on a roll of carpet, their eyes staring solemnly.

For a moment Tim was too fascinated to move. Then the street lamp, which the lorry had hit, suddenly toppled over with a crash.

A man in pyjamas appeared in the ruined doorway of the warehouse, his mouth open and his sleepy eyes peering about unbelievingly.

Tim turned and raced away.

As Tim moved, the man noticed him for the first time. 'Hey, you!' he called, and began running after him.

Chapter Seven

Nine, Nine, Nine

Tim went running down the street, nearly slipping several times in his wet wellingtons. He quickly drew ahead of the man who was hopping painfully along in his bare feet.

Tim turned the corner and glanced up at the name-plates – Glass Street and Thames Lane. He ran up another long, straight street. As he came to

the next corner, he heard the clatter of footsteps behind him.

'The others will be out now,' he thought. 'With shoes on, too. I must find a telephone soon.'

There were no turnings off this street. He was sobbing for breath now and a pain was gathering in his chest.

He glanced down the first side road. There was no telephone box, but at the end of the road between the black houses the River Thames was silver in the early morning light, and a line of silver shone in the sky.

Daylight was not far away and made Tim feel more hopeful. He ran on to the next turning faster still.

He swung round the corner and there in the distance was a telephone box. It glowed like a friendly red and gold lantern in the shadow of the tall warehouses.

The footsteps came still nearer, and Tim screwed up the remains of his energy for a last burst of speed.

His heart was thudding away inside him as if it were trying to escape from his body. Purple blobs floated in front of his eyes, and as he drew nearer, the glowing box seemed to sway dizzily from side to side.

He ran at the box with arms spread wide as if to catch it. Then his fingers grasped for the brass handle and he heaved with all his remaining strength at the heavy door.

Three men appeared in the distance and one shouted at him. The door opened a little and Tim practically fell inside. He picked up the receiver, pressed his finger into the nine and moved it round to the stop. The dial spun slowly back as the foot-steps pounded nearer. Nine again; slowly the dial spun back as Tim sobbed with impatience and the footsteps pounded like thunder. Once more, nine: – slowly, slowly, the dial crawled back.

'Emergency. What service are you calling?'

'What?' sobbed Tim, his head reeling.

'Fire, Police or Ambulance?'

'Police! Police!' cried Tim. 'Glass Street and Thames Lane!'

The receiver suddenly became very heavy in his hand, and Tim tried hard to lift it back into place, but a spinning blackness came rushing out of the roof of the box and he fell to the floor. The receiver dangled on its cord and swung gently to and fro above him.

TELEPHONE

A moment later the door was torn open by a burly man in vest and pyjama trousers. Tim's limp body rolled out on to the pavement. His eyes were closed and his face was pale and damp.

'The little devil!' fumed the burglar called Jim. 'I'd like to wring his neck. How the blazes did those kids get in?' He picked Tim up by his coat collar as if he had been a doll. 'How did you get in, you little perisher?' he roared, thrusting his bristly face into Tim's and shaking him.

'Taff's got the other one,' said a little fat man.

'What of it?' raged Jim. 'The game's up now. The cops will be here any minute. Let's get back for our clothes.'

He dropped Tim on to his feet and the three men turned and ran, leaving Tim dizzy and swaying.

A minute later, before they had even reached the first corner, a police car turned into the street at the far end. Its headlights were blazing and its siren wailing.

'Here they come!' shouted one of the men and they ran still faster. A moment later the car flashed

past Tim, raced up to the running men, mounted the pavement and skidded to a stop in front of them.

The doors of the police car opened and the fat burglar almost ran into the lap of the sergeant at the wheel. A tall constable unfolded himself from the car like a jack-knife opening, grabbed one of the burglars, and practically threw him straight into the back of the car.

The big, tough one swerved and ran back towards Tim, who was by now wide-awake again. Tim stood ready with head lowered and shoulders hunched.

'Out of my way, kid!' roared the man, but at that moment the cord at his waist came undone, his pyjamas slipped down to his ankles and he fell to the ground.

Tim and the policemen doubled up with laughter. Then two laughing constables came up, hauled the tough one to his feet and frog-marched him into the car, with his pyjamas still round his ankles and his face a bright red.

'Come on, son, you've got a lot of explaining to do,' said the smiling inspector as he came up to Tim and led him to the car.

In a few seconds they arrived back at the warehouse to find Taff feverishly trying to get all the stuff back inside the building. He had moved some of the furniture and was now trying to push the refrigerator up the kerb by himself.

The moment the car stopped Tim jumped out. 'Where's Gerry?' he asked.

'Who?' wheezed Taff, leaning on the refrigerator and gazing stupidly at the police car. He had still not quite understood what had happened, or what was happening now.

'Where's the other boy?' barked the inspector, seizing Taff by his pyjama jacket.

'Oh – er, sir, he's in the cupboard, sir,' mumbled Taff, saluting vaguely and trying to stand to attention.

'Great heavens, the man's a half-wit!' cried the inspector. 'Put him away, sergeant.'

Taff was bundled into the car on top of his friends, and the constable who had run into the warehouse came out with Gerry.

The inspector pushed his cap on to the back of his head, gestured helplessly towards the pile of furniture and wreckage, then turned to the two grinning boys. 'Now for goodness' sake, how did all this happen?'

Chapter Eight

The Major-General

Tim and Gerry were taken to the police station and they explained it all to the inspector over a gigantic breakfast of fried eggs and bacon, and big mugs of steaming tea.

'Mmm, that was good,' said Tim. 'Look, it's still only five in the morning; Sunday too.'

'We'd better telephone your parents,' said the inspector, 'then run you home. I shouldn't like to be in your shoes. I'd better come with you to help explain.'

Gerry's parents came round to Tim's house and they all met the inspector together. The parents were very annoyed with the boys for going out at night, but they calmed down a little when the inspector told them how brave they had been.

When the inspector had gone, Tim's mother said, 'You two must be starving, have you had anything to eat?'

'Er – yes, just a bite,' said Tim cautiously.

'I must get you something,' Mrs Rogers went on. 'How about eggs and bacon?'

In the middle of their feed a reporter and a photographer called. They took several pages of notes, and flash bulbs exploded all over the kitchen.

Tim and Gerry became so excited they almost forgot to go on eating.

'Won't it be good?' said Tim, helping himself to a big spoonful of marmalade. 'Headline News – Boys Catch Burglars. Prime Minister Congratulates. Knighthoods For Both Boys. Sir Gerald and Sir Timothy said yesterday –'

'Hi, steady on,' said his father. 'You may be in trouble yourselves yet. The golf club people may not like you using their lake without permission.'

'Oh, yes, that's right,' groaned Gerry. 'Our rods are still there.'

Tim and Gerry looked blankly at one another, their excitement gone.

So later that morning the two tired boys made their way back to the golf club.

'Well, here we go,' said Gerry, as they went through the gates. 'We're for it now.'

As they walked down the drive they saw a removal van and the stolen furniture being unloaded. A man in a loud check suit was shouting orders at the men unloading the van, and he turned round as he heard their footsteps on the gravel.

'Yes, what can I do for you?' he asked sharply,

his eyes piercing into them from under his frowning brows.

'We – we came about our rods –' Tim faltered.

'We were fishing here last night – sir,' said Gerry.

'Ha! So you're the little beggars are you? Trespassers! Poachers! Do you realize that this ground is private and that people pay a great deal of money for a licence to fish here? Do you? Eh?'

Tim and Gerry looked down at the ground, unable to say anything.

'The club is considering having you prosecuted with the full force of the law. You had better come inside with me.'

He wheeled round and stumped up the steps. Gerry and Tim shakily followed him, their legs feeling very weak, and their mouths beginning to go dry with fright. Some of the stolen furniture had

been put back, but the room still looked bare.

'Sit on those stools!'

The boys climbed on to the high stools and perched there awkwardly while the man moved about behind the bar. After a few moments he put down in front of them two tall glasses of golden shandy with red cherries and lumps of ice-cream floating on top.

At the sight of their astonished faces the man suddenly burst into laughter.

'Well, go on. Get on with it. I know it's not much like a Knickerbocker Glory, but it's the best I can do.'

Still laughing, he turned away and went out of the room.

Gerry and Tim looked dumbly at one another for a moment, then slowly picked up their spoons. They had almost finished when the man came back.

'Now, gentlemen,' he said. 'My name is General Clark and I am the Secretary of the club, so please allow me to present you with these on behalf of the members of the Park Lake Golf and Fishing Club.'

He laid on the bar two beautiful green rods.

Their gleaming rings were lined with orange-coloured agate, and were bound on with fine red twine. The smooth cork handles ended in a knob of shining silver.

'They're really our presentation rods for the best catch of the year,' the General went on, then added with a laugh: 'I think you've certainly won them for this year. And here are licences for you both so that you can fish in the lake whenever you wish.'

The boys stuttered out their thanks, then hesitantly picked up the rods as carefully as if they had been made of glass. A few moments later they walked clumsily down the steps of the club house, still in a daze.

'Don't bother about your own rods,' the General called after them. 'I'll have them sent down later. Good-bye to you.'

'Good-bye, sir,' called Tim and Gerry, turning back to wave.

As they walked up the drive, the fine tips of the rods dipped and waved against the blue sky. Huge, imaginary fish already tugged at their ends.

'Lovely rods,' said Gerry.

'Much better than knighthoods,' replied Tim.

Gerry agreed and twirled his rod happily in the air.

THE STRANGE HOUSE

Written and illustrated by Raymond Briggs

Tim and Gerry knew they should not be on the golf course. Running away from some angry golfers, they found themselves in the grounds of a strange house. Why is the house boarded up? Why does the fierce woman try to chase them away? And whose is the mysterious face at an upstairs window? The only way Tim and Gerry can find out is to get into the house . . . somehow . . .